I Like to Go to Church

Phyllis Boykin • Illustrated by **James Padgett**

Broadman Press
Nashville, Tennessee

To
my daughter, Cherie,
with love

© Copyright 1987 • Broadman Press
All rights reserved.
4241-74

ISBN: 0-8054-4174-3
Library of Congress Catalog Card Number: 86-17538
Dewey Decimal Classification: C262
Subject Heading: CHURCH

Printed in the United States of America

Library of Congress Cataloging-in-Publication Data

Boykin, Phyllis.
  I like to go to church.

  (Bible-and-me)
  Summary: Discusses the people at church who are
available for help, the ways in which they help, people
in the Bible who helped at church, and reasons for
being happy to be at church.
  1. Church—Juvenile literature   [1. Church]
I. Padgett, Jim, ill.   II. Title.   III. Series.
BV602.5.B69   1987   264   86-17538
ISBN 0-8054-4174-3

Cherie moved to a new house. She will have a new room. She will have new friends.

Cherie and Mother go for a walk. They see
houses and yards with green grass. "What
is that house?" asks Cherie.

"That is our new church," Mother says. "Is it like our other church?" Cherie asks. "Let's go see," Mother says.

"Hello, my name is Mr. Roberts." "This is Cherie," says Mother. "Is this your church?" Cherie asks.

"Yes, it is my church. I am the pastor. It can be your church too," says Mr. Roberts.
"Here is your room."

"This room is like my room at my old church," says Cherie. Mr. Roberts shows Cherie the books.

"This book tells about winter," he says.
"God made winter. He made spring and
summer. He made fall."

"Good-bye, Cherie," Mr. Roberts says.
"Come to church again." Cherie waves
good-bye.

"The Bible tells us Samuel went to church," says Mother. Cherie sees a picture of Samuel in her Bible.

On Sunday morning Daddy, Mother, and Cherie go to church. "I am going to a new church," says Cherie. "I will have new friends."

"Hello, Cherie. I am Mrs. Harris. I am one of your teachers. I am glad you came to church."

Cherie and her new friends play with blocks. "The Bible tells us to be kind," Mr. Harris says. "You are being kind."

Cherie has a new friend. His name is
George. Cherie and George are being
helpers. Mr. Harris has a book about
helpers.

"Samuel was a helper at church," Mr. Harris says. Cherie and her friends look at the picture of Samuel in the Bible.

"God made the animals," Mr. Harris says. Cherie sees an animal in the book. "God made animals," she says.

Mrs. Harris waves good-bye to Cherie.
Cherie likes her new friends. She likes her
new church.

Mother and Daddy are ready to go home. Cherie waves good-bye to George. She is glad she came to church.

Cherie holds Mother's hand. She holds
Daddy's hand. "I like to go to church,"
Cherie sings.

"We like to go to church too," say Mother and Daddy. "We like our new church."

On Sunday night Cherie and Mother and
Daddy go to church. "I am going to my
new church. I will see my new friends," says
Cherie.

"God made butterflies. God made seashells," says Miss Green. "We had a seashell in my old church," says Cherie.

"It is time to go home," say Mother and Daddy. "Good-bye Miss Green," says Cherie. "I will come to my new church again."

Mother and Daddy and Cherie go home. "I came to my new church two times," says Cherie. "My new church is like my old church."

Cherie goes to her new church during the week. Sometimes she paints a picture. "I like red paint. I like yellow paint," says Cherie.

Andy and Bill draw pictures. Mrs. Carter says, "You used red and yellow and blue. God made red flowers, yellow flowers, and a blue sky."

Cherie and a new friend, Mike, make music.
Mr. Denver listens. He says, "We can make
music at church."

Miss Anderson and Charlie and Susan listen to a song. "We can listen to a song at church," Miss Anderson says.

Mr. Roberts comes to visit Cherie and her family. "Come in Mr. Roberts," say Cherie and Mother. "We are glad to see you."

Cherie shows Mr. Roberts her Bible. "The Bible says I like to go to church," Mr. Roberts tells Cherie.

"I like to go to church. I like our new church," says Cherie. "Thank You, God, for our new church," say Mother and Daddy.